ONE DAY AT A TIME

BE AWARE OF NATURAL CATASTROPHES THAT CAN DESTROY HUMAN LIFE
LET US STOP THE ARTIFICIAL KILLING

WRITTEN BY DR. SANUBO TOEQUE, ED.D.
COVER DESIGN DR. KOFFAJUAH TOEQUE, ED.D.

ONE DAY AT A TIME

BE AWARE OF NATURAL CATASTROPHES THAT CAN DESTROY HUMAN LIFE
LET US STOP THE ARTIFICIAL KILLING

WRITTEN BY DR. SANUBO TOEQUE, ED. D.
COVER DESIGN DR. KOFFAJUAH TOEQUE, ED. D

ARPress
45 Dan Road Suite 15
Canton MA 02021
  Hotline: 1(888) 821-0229
  Fax: 1(508) 545-7580

Ordering Information:
Quantity sales. Special discounts are available on quantity purchases by corporations, associations, and others. For details, contact the publisher at the address above.

Printed in the United States of America.

  ISBN-13:   Softcover   979-8-89676-385-7
              eBook   979-8-89676-386-4

Library of Congress Control Number: 2025918476

TABLE OF CONTENTS

About the Author

The author, Dr. Sanubo Toeque, II was born in Harbel, Margibi, Liberia, West Africa. He is a Preacher/Evangelist for One Accord Educational Ministry (OAEM). A.S. degree Chemistry Bronx Community College of the City University of New York, B.S. degree Chemistry Pepperdine University, Malibu, California, M.A. degree Educational Administration California State University Dominguez Hills, Carson, California, M.S. Chemistry California Polytechnic University, Pomona, California, Ed. D Educational Leadership, Argosy University, Orange County, California, and M.S. Chemical Engineering California State University, Long Beach, California.

Forward

As we navigate the complexities of our rapidly changing world, the need for vigilance, compassion, and cooperation has never been greater. "One Day at a Time: Be Aware of Natural Catastrophes That Can Destroy Human Life - Let Us Stop the Artificial Killing" serves as a beacon of hope and a call to action in the face of natural disasters and human-induced destruction.

Through the pages of this book, readers will embark on a journey of discovery, learning about the diverse array of natural catastrophes that threaten human life and the underlying causes of environmental degradation. From earthquakes and hurricanes to deforestation and pollution, each chapter offers valuable insights and practical solutions for building resilience, promoting sustainability, and fostering a culture of environmental stewardship.

Preface

In a world where natural catastrophes and human-induced destruction loom large, it is essential to understand the intricate dynamics of our environment and the consequences of our actions. "One Day at a Time: Be Aware of Natural Catastrophes That Can Destroy Human Life - Let Us Stop the Artificial Killing" is a testament to the urgent need for awareness, preparedness, and collective action in the face of these pressing challenges.

This book delves into the science, impacts, and solutions related to natural disasters and human-induced destruction, aiming to empower readers with knowledge and insight to drive positive change. Through exploration of the causes, mechanisms, and impacts of natural catastrophes, as well as the ways in which human activities contribute to environmental degradation, this book seeks to shed light on the interconnectedness of these issues and inspire readers to take action to protect our planet and its inhabitants.

Chapter 1
The Fragile Balance - Explained

This chapter delves into the delicate equilibrium within Earth's ecosystems and the interconnectedness of all living organisms. It explores the concept of ecological balance and the intricate relationships between humans, wildlife, and the environment. Key themes include:

1. **Ecological Interdependence**
2. **Biodiversity and Ecosystem Health**
3. **Human Impacts on the Environment**
4. **Climate Change**
5. **Environmental Stewardship**
6. **Ethical and Moral Considerations**

The Introduction of Natural Catastrophes

Let's start delineating and providing familiar definitions of natural catastrophes.

Natural catastrophes can be categorized into several types, each characterized by its unique causes and mechanisms.

Types of Natural Catastrophes:

1. Earthquakes:

Figure 1.1 A Depiction of the *Northern California earthquake 6.4 magnitude*

- **Definition:** Earthquakes are sudden and violent shaking of the ground caused by the movement of tectonic plates beneath the Earth's surface.

- **Causes:** Earthquakes occur due to the release of stress accumulated along geological fault lines. This stress can build up over time as tectonic plates shift and collide.

- **Mechanisms:** When the stress along a fault exceeds the strength of the rocks holding it in place, the rocks fracture and slip, releasing energy in the form of seismic waves. These waves propagate through the Earth, causing the ground to shake.

2. Hurricanes and Cyclones:

Figure 1.2 **A Depiction of the *Outer Bands of Tropical Cyclones***

- **Definition:** Hurricanes (in the Atlantic and Northeast Pacific) and cyclones (in the Northwest Pacific) are powerful tropical storms characterized by strong winds, heavy rainfall, and storm surges.

- **Causes:** Hurricanes and cyclones form over warm ocean waters when atmospheric conditions are conducive to the development of thunderstorms and low-pressure systems.

- **Mechanisms:** Warm Ocean waters provide the energy needed to fuel the storm, causing moist air to rise and condense, releasing latent heat and forming clouds. As the storm intensifies, it generates strong winds and heavy rainfall, leading to flooding and coastal erosion.

3. Floods:

Figure 1.3 **A Depiction of the *Floods Catastrophes***

- **Definition:** Floods occur when an area of land becomes inundated with water, either due to heavy rainfall, overflowing rivers, storm surges, or rapid snowmelt.

- **Causes:** Floods can result from various factors, including prolonged rainfall, rapid snowmelt, dam failures, or the blocking of river channels by debris.

- **Mechanisms:** Excessive precipitation or snowmelt leads to an accumulation of water on the land surface, which overwhelms natural or man-made drainage systems, causing water to spread and inundate surrounding areas.

Project Title:

Smart Flash Flood Diversion System Using Pipes, Sensors, and Sirens for Urban Safety

1. **Executive Summary:**

   Flash flooding poses an increasing threat to urban communities due to climate change, urban sprawl, and inadequate drainage systems. This project proposes a **Smart Flood Diversion System** using **underground diversion pipes** equipped with **real-time water-level sensors** and **automated siren alerts.** The system detects rising floodwaters and redirects excess water to safe outflow locations such as rivers, retention basins, or oceans—while alerting residents with audible sirens.

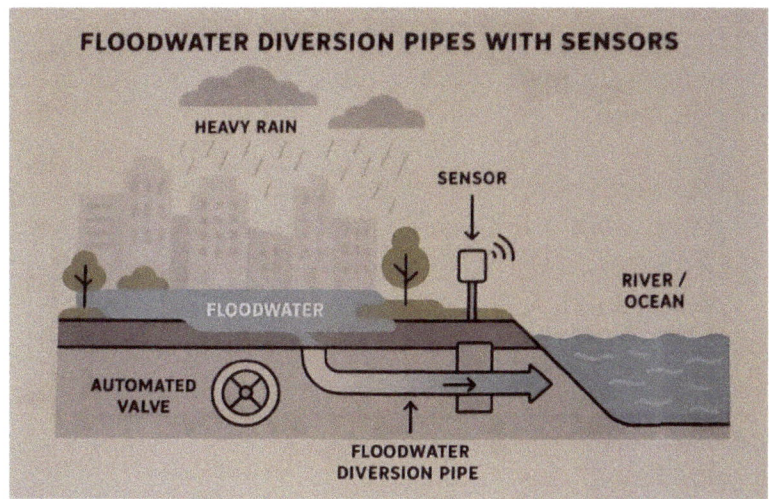

Figure 1.4 **A Depiction of the** *Floodwater Diversion Pipes with Sensors*

4. Wildfires:

Figure 1.5 **A Depiction of the** *Hawaii Wildfires*

- **Definition:** Wildfires are uncontrolled fires that spread rapidly through vegetation, forests, or grasslands, fueled by dry conditions, high temperatures, and strong winds.

- **Causes:** Wildfires can be ignited by lightning strikes, human activities such as campfires, discarded cigarettes, or arson, and can spread rapidly under favorable weather conditions.

- **Mechanisms:** Once ignited, wildfires spread through the combustion of vegetation, releasing heat and generating flames and embers that can travel long distances, igniting new fires.

Wildfire Suppression: An Innovative Approach to Fire Control Using Thermal Absorption.

As wildfires become more frequent and destructive due to climate change, current suppression tool—such as water drops and chemical retardants—have shown limitations in cost, availability, and environmental safety. Here is a revealed approach proposes the strategic deployment of crushed ice as **a non-toxic, thermally efficient alternative** to reduce fire intensity through latent heat absorption. By removing heat directly from fire zones, this method disrupts the fire. This is an innovative, thermodynamically based wildfire suppression strategy entitled **Crushed-Ice** fire triangle while minimizing ecological impact.

Mechanisms: How Crushed Ice Works to Suppress Wildfires

 1. **Initial Contact – Ice Meets Fire**

When **crushed ice is applied directly to burning vegetation or forest soil**, it:

- Immediately begins to **absorb thermal energy** from the flames and surrounding heat.

- Begins to **melt**, pulling in **latent heat of fusion**, which helps **lower the temperature rapidly** in burning zone.

- ❖ This **temperature drop** is often more effective than spraying liquid water alone, which can sometimes evaporate before cooling deeply.

 **Result**

1. **Heating Curve Analysis**

   The heating curve analysis confirmed that crushed ice exhibits substantial thermal absorption during its phase transitions. The temperature remained constant at **0°C during melting,** absorbing an average of **334 kJ/kg** (latent heat of fusion) before transitioning to water. As temperatures increased, water evaporated, absorbing an additional **2260 kJ/kg** (latent heat of vaporization).

Figure 1.6 displays the heating curve of crushed ice applied to a preheated fuel bed. The temperature drop following ice application was immediate and sustained, with surface temperatures falling from **450°C to below 120°C within 90 seconds,** delaying re-ignition.

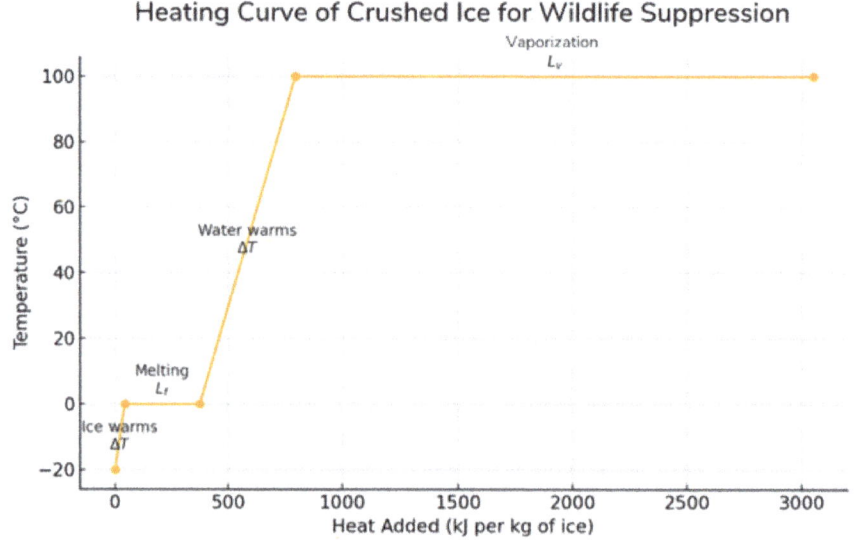

Figure 1.6 A Depiction of the *Heating Curve Analysis*

5. Tsunamis:

Figure 1.7 A Depiction of the *Tsunamis Catastrophe*

- **Definition:** Tsunamis are large ocean waves caused by underwater earthquakes, volcanic eruptions, landslides, or the collapse of underwater cliffs.

- **Causes:** Tsunamis are triggered by the sudden displacement of water, often as a result of tectonic activity or submarine landslides.

- **Mechanisms:** When an underwater disturbance occurs, it displaces a large volume of water, generating waves that propagate outward in all directions. As these waves approach shallow coastal areas, they can increase in height and cause devastating inundation.

6. Tornado:

Figure 1.8 **Comprehensive overview of tornados, including a visual representation, their definition, causes and mechanisms.**

- **Definition:** A tornado is a violently rotating column of air that extends from a thunderstorm to the ground. These phenomena are typically associated with cumulonimbus clouds and are characterized by their funnel-shaped appearance. Tornadoes can cause significant damage due to their high wind speeds and the debris they carry.

- **Causes:** Tornadoes primarily form under specific atmospheric conditions:

  - **Severe Thunderstorms:** Especially those known as supercells, which have a persistent rotating updraft called a mesocyclone.

- **Wind Shear:** variations in wind speed and direction at different altitudes create horizontal spinning air currents.

- **Atmospheric Instability:** When warm, moist air near the ground meets cooler, dry air above, it can lead to the development of strong updrafts.

- **Lift Mechanisms:** Features like cold fronts or dry lines can force warm air upward, initiating thunderstorm development.

- **Mechanisms:** The formation of a tornado involves several steps:

  1. **Horizontal Rotation:** Wind shear creates a horizontal spinning effect in the lower atmosphere.

  2. **Updraft Tilting:** Strong updrafts within a thunderstorm can tilt this horizontal *rotation into a vertical orientation*.

  3. **Mesocyclone Formation:** The vertically oriented rotating air forms a mesocyclone within the storm.

  4. **Tornado Development:** Under certain conditions, the mesocyclone's rotation tightens and intensifies, extending downward to form a tornado., or how tornadoes are classified using.

Chapter 2
Exploring the Causes and Mechanisms

Chapter 2 builds on the definitions and characteristics of natural catastrophes introduced in Chapter 1 by examining the underlying processes and environmental conditions that intensify these events. By understanding the broader factors and mechanisms driving these catastrophes, we gain valuable insights into how climate, geology, human activity, and ecosystem dynamics interact to shape the frequency, intensity, and impact of natural disasters. This chapter highlights the importance of predictive science and environmental awareness as tools to reduce vulnerability and enhance resilience.

1. Environmental and Climatic Factors Contributing to Natural Disasters

Natural catastrophes are often linked to specific environmental and climatic conditions. These factors can heighten the severity of a disaster, making certain regions more vulnerable to particular types of events.

Key environmental factors include:

- **Climate and Weather Patterns:** Shifts in climate and seasonal weather patterns can make regions more susceptible to extreme weather events. For instance, El Niño and La Niña phenomena influence ocean temperatures and atmospheric circulation, leading to cycles of intense rainfall or drought in various parts of the world.

- **Warming Oceans and Rising Sea Levels**: Ocean temperatures play a crucial role in the formation of hurricanes and cyclones. Warmer sea temperatures increase storm intensity, while rising sea levels make coastal regions more vulnerable to storm surges, exacerbating flooding during hurricanes and cyclones.

- **Dry and Arid Conditions**: Regions with prolonged dry seasons, low rainfall, and high temperatures are more prone to wildfires. The combination of dry vegetation and extreme heat creates an ideal environment for fires to ignite and spread rapidly.

Figure 2.1 A Depiction of *Exploring the Causes and Mechanisms*

2. Geological Processes: Tectonic and Volcanic Activity

The movement and interaction of Earth's tectonic plates drive many geological disasters, including earthquakes, tsunamis, and volcanic eruptions. Understanding these processes provides a foundation for assessing risk in tectonically active regions:

- **Plate Tectonics and Fault Lines:** Earth's lithosphere is divided into tectonic plates that move over the semi-fluid asthenosphere. Where these plates meet, stress builds up, and when it is released, earthquakes occur. Regions along tectonic boundaries, such as the Pacific Ring of Fire, are particularly susceptible to seismic and volcanic activity.

- **Subduction Zones and Volcanic Activity**: At convergent plate boundaries, one tectonic plate is forced under another in a process called subduction, creating pressure and heat that leads to magma formation. Subduction zones, such as those near Japan and the Andes Mountains, are common sites for volcanic eruptions and are associated with the creation of stratovolcanoes, which can produce highly explosive eruptions.

- **Seafloor Spreading and Rift Zones**: Divergent boundaries, where tectonic plates move apart, allow magma to rise and form new crust, as seen in mid-ocean ridges. These zones, while less explosive, contribute to seafloor spreading and occasionally generate undersea volcanic activity, which can trigger tsunamis if they involve a significant displacement of the ocean floor.

3. Human Impact and Environmental Degradation

Human activity has a significant influence on the frequency, intensity, and consequences of natural catastrophes. Rapid urbanization, deforestation, and climate change are some of the ways humans contribute to an increased risk of disasters:

- **Deforestation and Soil Erosion**: The removal of vegetation destabilizes soil, leading to erosion, increased landslide risk, and decreased water retention, which can exacerbate flood conditions during heavy rains.

- **Urbanization and Infrastructure Development**: Expanding cities often encroach on natural floodplains, coastal areas, and forests. This increases the population density in high-risk areas, limits natural drainage, and places critical infrastructure in vulnerable locations, compounding the effects of disasters like floods and hurricanes.

- **Greenhouse Gas Emissions and Climate Change**: Human-induced climate change, driven by greenhouse gas emissions, intensifies weather-related disasters. Rising global temperatures have led to an increase in the frequency and intensity of heatwaves, droughts, and hurricanes, and have altered precipitation patterns, causing extreme rainfall and prolonged dry seasons.

4. Ecosystem Interactions and Natural Feedback Loops

Natural ecosystems play a crucial role in mitigating or intensifying the effects of natural disasters. Ecosystem health and the balance of ecological interactions influence the severity of catastrophes:

- **Wetlands and Mangroves as Natural Buffers**: Wetlands and mangroves act as natural barriers against storms and flooding by absorbing excess water and dissipating wave energy. The degradation of these ecosystems increases the vulnerability of coastal areas to hurricanes, storm surges, and tsunamis.

- **Forests and Carbon Sequestration**: Forests absorb carbon dioxide from the atmosphere, helping to regulate global temperatures. When forests are destroyed, carbon is released, contributing to climate change. Additionally, the absence of forests makes regions more prone to soil erosion, landslides, and desertification.

- **Feedback Loops in Climate and Weather Systems**: Climate feedback mechanisms, such as the melting of polar ice caps, contribute to global warming and rising sea levels. Melting ice reduces Earth's albedo (reflectivity), causing more sunlight to be absorbed, which accelerates warming and creates a cycle of increasingly extreme weather patterns.

5. Technological and Predictive Tools for Understanding Catastrophes

Advances in technology have significantly improved our ability to understand, monitor, and predict natural disasters. These tools are essential for early warning systems, disaster preparedness, and mitigation strategies:

- **Seismic Monitoring and Early Warning Systems**: Seismographs and accelerometers detect and measure ground movement, allowing scientists to monitor earthquake activity and send early warnings. These systems are especially valuable in regions prone to tsunamis, where minutes of warning can save lives.

- **Satellite Imagery and Remote Sensing**: Satellites provide real-time data on weather patterns, sea temperatures, and forest cover, helping scientists track storms, monitor deforestation, and assess flood risks. Remote sensing also assists in damage assessment and resource allocation after a disaster.

- **Climate Modeling and Simulation:** Advanced climate models allow scientists to predict the frequency and severity of extreme weather events under different climate scenarios. These simulations help inform policies and preparedness efforts, guiding nations in adapting to a changing climate.

- **GIS and Hazard Mapping**: Geographic Information Systems (GIS) enable the mapping of high-risk areas for earthquakes, floods, and landslides. Hazard maps, which integrate historical data and environmental factors, help planners make informed decisions about land use, construction, and evacuation routes.

6. Socioeconomic and Cultural Dimensions of Natural Disasters

Natural catastrophes disproportionately impact vulnerable populations, revealing the importance of understanding socioeconomic and cultural factors:

- **Social Vulnerability and Access to Resources**: Communities with limited economic resources and infrastructure are less able to prepare for and recover from natural disasters. Socioeconomic factors, such as income inequality and education, influence a community's ability to implement resilience measures.

- **Cultural Attitudes and Disaster Preparedness**: Different cultures have varying beliefs about natural disasters, which can affect how communities approach preparedness. For instance, some cultures view certain disasters as acts of fate, which may reduce proactive disaster planning. Recognizing cultural dimensions are essential for designing effective, inclusive risk-reduction strategies.

- **Population Density and Migration**: Urban centers with high population density faces greater challenges in evacuating residents and ensuring adequate emergency resources. Climate change and disaster-prone conditions are also leading to increased migration, as people are forced to relocate from high-risk areas, creating complex socioeconomic and political challenges.

Conclusion

"Exploring the Causes and Mechanisms" provides a deeper understanding of the broader factors that influence natural catastrophes. By examining environmental conditions, human impact, ecosystem interactions, technological advancements, and socioeconomic dimensions, this chapter presents a comprehensive view of the complexity underlying natural disasters. Armed with this knowledge, we can better predict, prepare for, and mitigate the impacts of these catastrophic events, paving the way toward a more resilient future.

Chapter 3
A Depiction of the Wrath of Nature – Explored

Nature, with all its beauty and majesty, also possesses a formidable power to unleash devastation upon human civilization. From the sudden fury of earthquakes and volcanic eruptions to the relentless force of hurricanes and typhoons, natural disasters have shaped the course of history and tested the resilience of societies around the world.

In this chapter, we confront the raw power of nature and the catastrophic impacts of its wrath on human lives, livelihoods, and infrastructure. We recount harrowing tales of survival and resilience in the face of disaster, as communities grapple with the aftermath of earthquakes that reduce cities to rubble in chapter 2, "Wrath of Nature Explored," delves into the intricate relationship between human civilization and the forces of nature.

It examines the impact of natural catastrophes on societies, economies, and the environment, exploring the ways in which communities respond to and recover from these events. Here are some key aspects explored in this chapter:

1. **Nature's Fury:** The chapter begins by illustrating the immense power of natural disasters, including hurricanes, earthquakes, tsunamis, wildfires, floods, and volcanic eruptions. It describes the devastation caused by these events, from loss of life and property damage to environmental destruction and economic disruption.

2. **Human Vulnerability**: Despite advances in science and technology, humans remain vulnerable to the whims of nature. The chapter examines the factors that contribute to human vulnerability, including population growth, urbanization, environmental degradation, and climate change. It highlights the disproportionate impact of natural disasters on marginalized communities, emphasizing the need for equitable disaster preparedness and response efforts.

Figure 3.1 Depiction of *Human Vulnerability*

3. **Resilience and Adaptation:** Despite the destructive power of natural disasters, human societies have demonstrated remarkable resilience and adaptability in the face of adversity. The chapter explores the strategies that communities employ to mitigate the impact of disasters, including early warning systems, evacuation plans, disaster relief efforts, and infrastructure improvements. It also examines the role of education, training, and public awareness campaigns in building resilience and fostering community cohesion.

4. **Environmental Consequences:** Natural disasters can have far-reaching environmental consequences, including habitat destruction, loss of biodiversity, soil erosion, water contamination, and air pollution. The chapter explores the ecological impacts of disasters and

the challenges of restoring ecosystems and mitigating environmental degradation in their aftermath.

5. **Global Perspectives**: The chapter takes a global perspective on natural disasters, examining their occurrence and impact in different regions of the world. It explores the disparities in disaster risk and vulnerability between developed and developing countries, as well as the role of international cooperation and humanitarian aid in responding to global crises.

6. **Lessons Learned**: Finally, the chapter reflects on the lessons learned from past disasters and the importance of integrating these insights into disaster risk reduction and management policies. It emphasizes the need for interdisciplinary approaches that combine scientific expertise, community engagement, policy advocacy, and grassroots initiatives to build resilience and foster sustainable development in an uncertain world.

Figure 3.2 Depiction of *Lessons Learned*

Overall, "Wrath of Nature Explored" offers a comprehensive exploration of the complex dynamics between humans and the natural world, highlighting both the challenges and opportunities inherent in navigating an increasingly volatile and unpredictable environment. e, tsunamis that engulf coastlines in a wall of water, and wildfires that consume vast swathes of forest and homes.

Chapter 4
The Impacts of Natural Catastrophes

Natural catastrophes have profound and often devastating impacts on human lives, infrastructure, economies, and ecosystems. In this chapter, we explore the wide-ranging consequences of natural disasters and examine real-life examples of communities affected by these catastrophic events.

Devastating Impacts on Human Lives:

Natural catastrophes can result in the loss of human lives, injuries, displacement, and profound psychological trauma. The sudden and violent nature of events such as earthquakes, hurricanes, and tsunamis can lead to widespread destruction and human suffering. Lives may be lost due to collapsing buildings, drowning, or injuries caused by flying debris. Displaced populations face challenges such as lack of shelter, clean water, and medical care, exacerbating their vulnerability.

Impact on Infrastructure:

Natural disasters often cause extensive damage to infrastructure, including buildings, roads, bridges, and utilities. Earthquakes can topple buildings, rupture pipelines, and disrupt transportation networks, while floods can inundate cities, wash away roads, and damage critical infrastructure such as power plants and water treatment facilities. The destruction of infrastructure hampers emergency response efforts impedes access to essential services and prolongs the recovery process.

Economic Consequences:

The economic impacts of natural catastrophes can be staggering, affecting local economies, national budgets, and global markets. Direct costs include property damage, loss of productivity, and expenditures on emergency response and recovery efforts. Indirect costs may arise from disruptions to supply chains, reduced tourism revenues, and long-term environmental degradation. Natural disasters can push individuals and communities into poverty and exacerbate existing socio-economic inequalities.

Figure 4.1 A Depiction of *Economic Consequences due to Environment Issues*

Ecological Damage:

Natural catastrophes can cause significant harm to ecosystems, biodiversity, and natural resources. Forest fires destroy habitats, disrupt wildlife populations and degrade air and water quality. Hurricanes and tsunamis can devastate coastal ecosystems, including coral reefs, mangroves, and wetlands, which provide vital ecosystem services such as coastal protection and habitat for marine life. Pollution and habitat destruction further threaten the resilience of ecosystems and the species that depend on them.

Real-Life Examples and Case Studies:

To illustrate the profound impacts of natural catastrophes, we examine real-life examples of communities affected by these events:

Figure 4.2: A Depiction of the *Haiti Quake 7.0 Jan 2010*

- The 2010 Haiti earthquake, which caused widespread devastation in the capital city of Port-au-Prince, resulting in over 200,000 deaths, extensive damage to infrastructure, and long-term humanitarian crises.

Figure 4.3 **A Depiction of** *a Hurricane*

- Hurricane Katrina, which struck the Gulf Coast of the United States in 2005, causing catastrophic flooding in New Orleans and the displacement of hundreds of thousands of residents, highlighting systemic failures in disaster preparedness and response.

- The 2011 Tohoku earthquake and tsunami in Japan, which triggered a nuclear disaster at the Fukushima Daiichi power plant, leading to radiation leaks, mass evacuations, and long-term environmental and health impacts.

Figure 4.4 A Depiction of the *Japan Earthquake and Tsunami 2011*

- The ongoing impacts of climate change, including more frequent and intense heat waves, droughts, and storms, which disproportionately affect vulnerable communities and exacerbate existing social and environmental challenges.

These examples underscore the urgent need for proactive measures to mitigate the impacts of natural catastrophes, strengthen resilience, and build more sustainable and inclusive societies. By understanding the far-reaching consequences of natural disasters, we can mobilize collective action to protect lives, livelihoods, and the planet for future generations.

Chapter 5

Understanding the Risks - Expounded

Chapter 5, "Understanding the Risks," offers an in-depth examination of the multifaceted risks that shape our modern world, focusing on their types, origins, and impacts on individuals, communities, and societies. It delves into the intricacies of risk categorization, explores root causes and factors that intensify these risks, and considers how vulnerabilities and resilience strategies can influence outcomes. This chapter also addresses the importance of ethical considerations, risk assessment tools, and global perspectives, providing a comprehensive view of the essential steps toward effective risk management.

1. Types of Risks

The chapter begins by categorizing risks into distinct yet interconnected types that often overlap and intensify each other's impact:

- **Natural Hazards**: These include earthquakes, floods, hurricanes, volcanic eruptions, and other geophysical events. The chapter explores the science behind these hazards, such as tectonic shifts, atmospheric conditions, and climate patterns, that create conditions for natural disasters. Recognizing their patterns and potential impacts are essential for forecasting and preparedness.

- **Technological Hazards**: Risks arising from human-made systems and technologies, such as industrial accidents, chemical spills, nuclear disasters, and cyber risks, are examined. The chapter highlights how technological progress, while beneficial, introduces new risks that require specialized management approaches, including safety regulations, cybersecurity protocols, and crisis response plans.

- **Environmental Hazards**: Risks stemming from environmental degradation, such as pollution, deforestation, and climate change, present long-term challenges. The chapter discusses how human activities can destabilize ecosystems, intensify climate change effects, and increase the occurrence of extreme weather events.

- **Social Risks**: Social issues, including poverty, inequality, conflict, and systemic discrimination, can create significant risks for individuals and communities. Social risks often compound with other risk types, making marginalized communities particularly vulnerable to natural and man-made disasters.

- **Health Risks:** Pandemics, infectious diseases, and public health crises highlight the intersection of biological and social factors. The chapter explores the global nature of health risks and the importance of surveillance, health infrastructure, and preventive measures in managing their spread.

Figure 5.1 A Depiction of *Types of Risk*

2. Risk Factors and Drivers

Understanding the drivers behind risks is key to identifying and managing them effectively. The chapter explores how interconnected factors can amplify risks and create cascading effects:

- **Population Growth and Urbanization**: Rapid population growth and urban expansion increase the density of people and infrastructure in vulnerable areas. Urbanization, especially in informal settlements, often leads to inadequate infrastructure, increasing susceptibility to hazards.

- **Globalization**: While globalization fosters economic interdependence, it also introduces risks, as disruptions in one region can cascade across the globe. Supply chain vulnerabilities, for example, became evident during health crises, underscoring the need for resilient systems.

Figure 5.2 **A Depiction of** *Globalization*

- **Economic Inequality**: Socioeconomic disparities amplify vulnerability to risks, as low-income populations often lack access to resources needed for risk mitigation. Economic inequality also influences recovery capacity, leading to prolonged hardship for the most disadvantaged.

- **Political Instability and Conflict**: Political factors, including governance challenges, corruption, and conflicts, can exacerbate risks, as governments may lack the stability or resources needed to implement effective risk management strategies.

- **Environmental Degradation**: Human activities, such as deforestation, mining, and industrial pollution, degrade natural environments, making ecosystems less resilient and amplifying the likelihood of environmental hazards, including climate change-induced events.

- **Technological Advancements**: Technological progress, while often beneficial, introduces new risks, such as cybersecurity threats, AI-related ethical dilemmas, and reliance on complex systems that may fail unexpectedly.

Figure 5.3 A Depiction of *Technological* Advancements

3. Vulnerability and Resilience

Vulnerability and resilience are central to understanding how risks impact different populations. This section highlights the factors that influence susceptibility to risks and outlines strategies to build resilience:

- **Vulnerability Factors**: Poverty, lack of access to resources, inadequate infrastructure, social marginalization, and limited education contributes to heightened vulnerability. Recognizing these factors are crucial for developing targeted risk reduction initiatives.

- **Building Resilience**: Resilience is defined as the capacity to withstand and recover from adverse events. Strategies to build resilience includes strengthening social networks, enhancing adaptive capacity and investing in protective infrastructure. Community-based approaches, local knowledge integration, and skill-building initiatives play essential roles in fostering resilience.

- **Social Resilience**: Resilience extends beyond physical infrastructure to include social factors. Strong social networks, community solidarity, and mental health support systems are vital for helping communities respond to and recover from disasters.

4. Risk Assessment and Management

Effective risk assessment and management require systematic approaches to identify, analyze, and respond to potential hazards. The chapter delves into both traditional and innovative tools and methods:

- **Risk Assessment Tools**: Hazard mapping, scenario planning, probabilistic modeling, and cost-benefit analysis are key tools for evaluating risks. These tools provide insights into potential impacts, helping planners allocate resources and prioritize risk reduction measures.

- **Participatory Approaches**: Engaging communities and stakeholders in the risk assessment process fosters trust, enhances local relevance, and ensures that diverse perspectives are considered. This inclusivity is essential for creating strategies that effectively address the needs and concerns of all affected groups.

- **Risk Mitigation Strategies**: Risk management requires proactive measures, such as policy development, regulatory enforcement, infrastructure investment, and contingency planning. Each approach aims to reduce exposure, minimize impacts, and facilitate recovery.

5. Ethical and Moral Dimensions

Risk management is not solely a technical or logistical challenge; it also involves profound ethical and moral considerations:

- **Justice and Equity:** Ethical risk management requires attention to justice and equity, particularly in resource distribution, risk allocation, and prioritizing the needs of vulnerable populations. The chapter discusses the ethical obligation to protect marginalized communities and future generations from disproportionate harm.

- **Intergenerational Responsibility**: Decisions made today have long-lasting impacts on future generations. Ethical risk management involves considering the legacy left for future populations and taking responsibility for sustainable practices that protect both current and future interests.

- **Risk Allocation and Responsibility**: Who should bear the burden of risk and who benefits from mitigation efforts are key ethical questions. The chapter explores these dilemmas, emphasizing the need for fair policies that distribute resources equitably and responsibly.

6. Global and Local Perspectives

Understanding risks requires both global and local lenses, as many risks have transboundary implications and demand international cooperation:

- **Transboundary Risks**: Climate change, pandemics, and geopolitical conflicts are examples of risks that cross borders. The chapter highlights the importance of global frameworks, such as international treaties and cooperative initiatives, to address these complex, interconnected risks effectively.

- **Importance of Local Context**: While global cooperation is essential, risk management strategies must also be tailored to specific local contexts. The chapter stresses the value of local knowledge, cultural considerations, and community priorities in developing effective, context-sensitive approaches.

- **International Cooperation and Solidarity**: Addressing risks often requires shared resources, information, and expertise across countries. This section examines the role of international organizations and alliances, such as the United Nations and regional coalitions, in fostering collaborative solutions to global challenges.

Conclusion

"Understanding the Risks" provides a comprehensive exploration of the complex, interwoven nature of risks that characterize the modern world. By categorizing risks, examining root causes, and emphasizing the importance of resilience, ethical responsibility, and collaborative approaches, this chapter underscores the need for holistic, inclusive risk management. Through an integrated approach that combines scientific expertise, social considerations, and ethical principles, societies can move towards a more resilient and sustainable future.

Chapter 6
Human-Induced Destruction: Causes and Consequences

Chapter 6, "Human-Induced Destruction," delves into the myriad ways in which human activities have contributed to environmental degradation and ecosystem destruction. It explores the various forms of anthropogenic impact on the environment, the underlying drivers of these destructive behaviors, and the consequences for ecosystems, biodiversity, and human well-being. Here's a detailed examination of the key themes addressed in this chapter:

1. **Deforestation:** The chapter begins by examining the widespread destruction of forests worldwide due to deforestation. It explores the drivers of deforestation, including agricultural expansion, logging, infrastructure development, and urbanization. It also discusses the ecological and socio-economic consequences of deforestation, such as loss of biodiversity, soil erosion, disruption of ecosystem services, and displacement of indigenous communities.

2. **Habitat Destruction:** Human activities have led to the destruction and fragmentation of natural habitats, threatening the survival of countless plant and animal species. The chapter explores the impacts of habitat destruction on biodiversity, including habitat loss, habitat degradation, and habitat fragmentation. It discusses the importance of protected areas, habitat restoration, and land-use planning in conserving and restoring critical habitats.

3. **Pollution:** Pollution is a significant driver of environmental degradation, affecting air, water, and soil quality. The chapter examines different types of pollution, including air pollution (from industrial emissions, vehicle exhaust, and agricultural practices), water pollution from industrial discharge, agricultural runoff, and improper waste disposal), and soil pollution (from heavy metals, pesticides, and industrial chemicals). It discusses the health impacts of pollution on humans and ecosystems and explore strategies for pollution prevention and remediation.

4. **Climate Change:** Human-induced climate change is one of the most pressing environmental challenges of our time. The chapter explores the causes and consequences of climate change, including greenhouse gas emissions from burning fossil fuels, deforestation, and industrial processes. It discusses the impacts of climate change on weather patterns, sea level rise, extreme weather events, and ecosystem stability. It also examines mitigation strategies, such as transitioning to renewable energy

sources, improving energy efficiency, and enhancing carbon sequestration.

5. Resource Depletion: Human activities have led to the depletion of natural resources, including freshwater, fisheries, minerals, and fossil fuels. The chapter explores the drivers of resource depletion, such as overexploitation, unsustainable consumption patterns, and population growth. It discusses the consequences of resource depletion for ecosystems, economies, and human societies and explores strategies for sustainable resource management, including conservation, renewable resource development, and circular economy approaches.

6. Social and Economic Drivers: Finally, the chapter examines the underlying social and economic drivers of human-induced destruction, including population growth, consumption patterns, economic development, globalization, and technological advancement. It discusses the role of governance, policy, and international cooperation in addressing these drivers and promoting more sustainable and equitable forms of development.

Overall, "Human-Induced Destruction" provides a comprehensive examination of the multifaceted ways in which human activities have contributed to environmental degradation and ecosystem decline. It underscores the urgent need for transformative action to address these challenges and transition to more sustainable and regenerative forms of development that promotes the well-being of both people and the planet.

Human activities have significantly contributed to environmental degradation, climate change, and the exacerbation of natural disasters. In this chapter, we examine the various ways in which human actions impact the environment and explore the far-reaching consequences of human-induced destruction on ecosystems, biodiversity, and the well-being of future generations.

Causes of Human-Induced Destruction:

1. Deforestation:

- Deforestation, driven by agricultural expansion, logging, and urbanization, results in the clearing of forests and the loss of critical habitat for wildlife. Deforestation reduces biodiversity, disrupts ecosystems, and contributes to climate change by releasing carbon stored in trees into the atmosphere.

2. Pollution:

- Industrial activities, transportation, agriculture, and waste disposal contribute to pollution of air, water, and soil. Air pollution from emissions of pollutants such as carbon dioxide (CO_2), sulfur dioxide (SO_2), and nitrogen oxides (NOx) contribute to climate change and respiratory illnesses. Water pollution from chemicals, sewage, and runoff harms aquatic ecosystems and human health.

3. Climate Change:

- Greenhouse gas emissions from burning fossil fuels, deforestation, and industrial processes are the primary drivers of climate change. The resulting increase in global temperatures leads to more frequent and intense heatwaves, droughts, storms, and sea-level rise, exacerbating the risks of natural disasters such as wildfires, hurricanes, and floods.

4. Urbanization:

- Rapid urbanization leads to the expansion of cities and the conversion of natural landscapes into built environments. Urbanization increases the demand for resources, energy, and infrastructure, resulting in habitat destruction, loss of biodiversity, and the fragmentation of ecosystems.

Consequences of Human-Induced Destruction:

1. Loss of Biodiversity:

- Human-induced destruction threatens biodiversity by reducing habitat availability, fragmenting ecosystems, and driving species extinction. Loss of biodiversity weakens ecosystem resilience, disrupts ecosystem services, and diminishes the ability of ecosystems to adapt to environmental changes.

2. Degradation of Ecosystems:

- Human activities degrade ecosystems through habitat destruction, pollution, overexploitation of natural resources, and introduction of invasive species. Degraded ecosystems provide fewer benefits to society, including clean air and water, food security, and climate regulation.

3. Impacts on Human Health:

- Human-induced destruction has direct and indirect impacts on human health. Air and water pollution contribute to respiratory diseases, cardiovascular diseases, and waterborne illnesses. Climate change exacerbates heat-related illnesses, vector-borne diseases, and food insecurity.

4. Threats to Future Generations:

- Human-induced destruction poses significant threats to the well-being of future generations by depleting natural resources, degrading ecosystems, and altering the climate system. Addressing these threats requires urgent action to transition to sustainable and resilient systems that prioritize environmental protection, social equity, and economic prosperity.

Exploring the causes and consequences of human-induced destruction underscores the urgent need for transformative action to address the root causes of environmental degradation, mitigate the impacts of climate change and promote sustainability and resilience. By recognizing the interconnectedness of human activities and their impacts on ecosystems and future generations, we can work towards a more sustainable and equitable future for all.

Chapter 7
Building Resilience: Preparedness and Mitigation

Building resilience and preparedness to natural disasters is essential for minimizing their impacts and protecting lives, infrastructure, and ecosystems. In this chapter, we outline strategies for enhancing resilience and preparedness, including the implementation of early warning systems, disaster response plans, infrastructure improvements, sustainable development practices, and ecosystem restoration efforts.

1. Early Warning Systems:

- Early warning systems play a critical role in alerting communities to impending natural disasters, providing valuable time for evacuation, preparedness, and response efforts. These systems utilize technologies such as seismometers, weather satellites, and monitoring networks to detect and forecast earthquakes, hurricanes, floods, and other hazards. By investing in the development and implementation of early warning systems, governments and organizations can save lives and minimize the impacts of natural disasters.

2. Disaster Response Plans:

- Disaster response plans outline coordinated actions and protocols for responding to natural disasters, including evacuation procedures, emergency shelters, medical care, and search and rescue operations. These plans involve collaboration between government agencies, emergency services, community organizations, and the private sector. By developing and regularly updating disaster response plans, communities can ensure a swift and effective response to natural disasters, reducing casualties and property damage.

3. Infrastructure Improvements:

- Strengthening infrastructure resilience is essential for mitigating the impacts of natural disasters and maintaining essential services during emergencies. Infrastructure improvements may include retrofitting buildings to withstand earthquakes, reinforcing bridges and roads to withstand floods and hurricanes, and upgrading utilities to enhance resilience to climate-related hazards. By investing in resilient infrastructure, communities can reduce vulnerability and enhance their capacity to withstand and recover from natural disasters.

4. Sustainable Development Practices:

-   Sustainable development practices promote long-term resilience by integrating environmental, social, and economic considerations into planning and decision-making processes. These practices emphasize principles such as resource efficiency, renewable energy, green infrastructure, and ecosystem-based approaches to disaster risk reduction. By adopting sustainable development practices, communities can reduce their vulnerability to natural disasters, enhance their adaptive capacity, and promote sustainable and inclusive growth.

5. Ecosystem Restoration:

-   Ecosystem restoration efforts, such as reforestation, wetland restoration, and coastal habitat conservation, can help mitigate the impacts of natural disasters by enhancing ecosystem services such as flood protection, erosion control, and water purification. Healthy ecosystems act as natural buffers against hazards, absorbing excess water, stabilizing soils, and reducing the intensity of storms. By restoring and protecting ecosystems, communities can enhance their resilience to natural disasters while conserving biodiversity and supporting livelihoods.

Chapter 8
Collaboration and Compassion - Explain

Chapter 8, "Collaboration and Compassion," delves into the importance of collective action and empathy in addressing social and environmental challenges. It explores the power of collaboration, solidarity, and compassion in building resilient communities, fostering positive social change and promoting sustainable development. Here's a detailed explanation of the key themes addressed in this chapter:

1. The Power of Collaboration: Collaboration involves individuals, organizations, and communities working together to achieve common goals and address shared challenges. The chapter highlights the importance of collaboration in tackling complex issues such as poverty, inequality, environmental degradation, and climate change. It explores examples of successful collaborations, including public-private partnerships, community-based initiatives, and multi-stakeholder coalitions, that have made significant progress in addressing social and environmental problems.

2. Collective Action and Social Change: Collective action refers to coordinated efforts by groups of individuals or organizations to achieve a common objective. The chapter examines the role of collective action in driving social change and promoting justice, equity, and human rights. It explores different forms of collective action, including grassroots organizing, advocacy campaigns, social movements, and protests, and discusses the strategies and tactics employed by activists to mobilize support and effect change.

3. Empathy and Compassion: Empathy is the ability to understand and share the feelings of others, while compassion is the desire to alleviate the suffering of others and promote their well-being. The chapter emphasizes the importance of empathy and compassion in fostering solidarity, building inclusive communities, and promoting social cohesion. It explores the role of empathy in fostering understanding and reconciliation across diverse perspectives and the importance of compassion in driving philanthropy, volunteerism, and altruistic behavior.

4. Building Resilient Communities: Resilient communities are those that are able to withstand and recover from adversity, such as natural disasters, economic downturns, or social crises. The chapter discusses the characteristics of resilient communities, including social cohesion, adaptive capacity, and resourcefulness, and explores the role of collaboration and compassion in building resilience. It examines community-based approaches to resilience-building, such as participatory planning, disaster preparedness, and social support networks, that empower individuals and communities to cope with and adapt to change.

5. Environmental Justice and Equity: Collaboration and compassion are essential for promoting environmental justice and equity, ensuring that all individuals and communities have access to clean air, water, and natural resources. The chapter examines environmental injustices, such as pollution burdens disproportionately borne by marginalized communities, and explores strategies for addressing environmental inequality through community-led initiatives, policy advocacy, and legal action.

6. Global Solidarity and Cooperation: Finally, the chapter explores the importance of global solidarity and cooperation in addressing transnational challenges such as climate change, biodiversity loss, and pandemic diseases. It emphasizes the need for international collaboration, resource sharing, and mutual support to tackle shared threats and achieve shared goals for a more sustainable and equitable world.

Overall, "Collaboration and Compassion" underscores the transformative potential of collective action and empathy in addressing pressing social and environmental issues. It highlights the importance of building strong, resilient communities grounded in principles of solidarity, inclusivity, and compassion, and calls for a renewed commitment to collaboration and cooperation at local, national, and global levels to create a more just, equitable, and sustainable future for all.

By implementing these strategies for building resilience and preparedness, communities can reduce their vulnerability to natural disasters, protect lives and livelihoods, and promote sustainable development. However, effective disaster risk reduction requires collaboration, investment, and commitment from governments, organizations, and individuals at all levels. By working together, we can build a more resilient and sustainable future for generations to come.

In the face of natural catastrophes and human-induced destruction, collaboration, compassion, and cooperation are indispensable pillars for building resilience, promoting sustainability, and fostering a sense of solidarity among communities and nations. In this chapter, we explore the transformative power of collaboration, the importance of compassion in times of crisis, and the benefits of cooperation in addressing shared challenges.

1. Collaboration:

- Collaboration involves working together across sectors, disciplines, and borders to achieve common goals and solve complex problems. In the context of natural disasters and environmental challenges, collaboration enables governments, organizations, communities, and individuals to pool resources, share knowledge, and coordinate efforts for disaster preparedness, response, and recovery. By fostering collaboration, we can harness collective expertise, leverage strengths, and maximize the impact of our actions in building resilience and mitigating the impacts of natural catastrophes.

2. Compassion:

- Compassion is the capacity to empathize with others and take action to alleviate their suffering. In times of crisis, compassion is powerful force for mobilizing support, providing aid, and offering comfort to those affected by natural disasters. Compassionate responses to disasters include acts of kindness, generosity, and solidarity, as well as efforts to address the root causes of vulnerability and promote social justice. By cultivating compassion in our communities and institutions, we can foster resilience, healing, and unity in the face of adversity.

3. Cooperation:

- Cooperation involves working together in a spirit of mutual respect, trust, and reciprocity to achieve shared objectives. In the context of environmental conservation and disaster risk reduction, cooperation among nations, regions, and stakeholders is essential for addressing transboundary challenges, sharing resources, and promoting sustainable development. International cooperation mechanisms, such as multilateral agreements, regional partnerships, and collaborative research initiatives, facilitate the exchange of best practices, technology transfer, and capacity-building efforts. By promoting cooperation, we can amplify our collective impact, enhance resilience, and build a more sustainable and equitable future for all.

4. Building Bridges:

- Building bridges across divides, whether they be geographical, cultural, or ideological, is essential for fostering collaboration, compassion, and cooperation in addressing environmental and humanitarian challenges. By transcending barriers and embracing diversity, we can build stronger, more inclusive communities and societies that are better equipped to respond to the complex and interconnected threats facing our planet. Building bridges also involves reaching out to marginalized and vulnerable populations, amplifying their voices, and ensuring their participation in decision-making processes.

Chapter 9
A Call to Action:
Collaboration and Cooperation

This Chapter serves as a rallying cry for individuals, communities, and nations to come together in addressing pressing global challenges. It emphasizes the importance of collective action, collaboration, and cooperation in overcoming barriers and achieving shared goals for a more sustainable and equitable world. Here's a detailed explanation of the key themes addressed in this chapter:

1. Urgent Global Challenges: The chapter begins by highlighting the urgency of the global challenges facing humanity, including climate change, biodiversity loss, poverty, inequality, and conflict. It underscores the interconnectedness of these challenges and their far-reaching impacts on people and the planet. It emphasizes the need for coordinated and decisive action to address these issues before they reach irreversible tipping points.

2. The Power of Collaboration: Collaboration involves individuals, organizations, and governments working together to tackle shared problems and achieve common objectives. The chapter explores the transformative potential of collaboration in driving positive change at local, national, and global levels. It examines examples of successful collaborations, such as international agreements like the Paris Agreement on climate change, and grassroots movements like the Fridays for Future climate strikes, that have mobilized collective action and galvanized public support for urgent issues.

3. Building Partnerships: Effective collaboration requires building strong partnerships and networks across sectors, disciplines, and geographic boundaries. The chapter discusses the importance of partnerships between governments, civil society organizations, businesses, academia, and communities in addressing complex challenges. It explores different models of partnership, such as public-private partnerships, multi-stakeholder initiatives, and community-based collaborations, that leverage diverse expertise, resources, and perspectives to drive innovation and scale impact.

4. Promoting Cooperation: Cooperation involves nations and regions working together to achieve shared objectives and address common threats. The chapter examines the role of international cooperation in promoting peace, security, and sustainable development. It discusses the importance of diplomacy, dialogue, and multilateralism in resolving conflicts, preventing armed conflicts, and fostering cooperation on issues such as disarmament, human rights, and global health.

5. Empowering Individuals and Communities: Collaboration and cooperation is not only about forging partnerships between institutions but also, about empowering individuals and communities to drive change from the bottom up. The chapter explores strategies for empowering grassroots movements, civil society organizations, and marginalized communities to participate in decision-making processes, advocate for their rights and hold governments and corporations accountable. It emphasizes the importance of inclusive and participatory approaches that amplify diverse voices and perspectives.

6. The Role of Leadership: Leadership plays a crucial role in fostering collaboration and cooperation and mobilizing collective action for positive change. The chapter examines the qualities of effective leadership, such as vision, integrity, empathy, and inclusivity, and explores the role of leaders in inspiring and mobilizing others to work towards common goals. It calls for bold and visionary leadership at all levels, from local community leaders to global statesmen, to navigate the complex challenges of the 21st century.

Overall, "A Call to Action: Collaboration and Cooperation" urges individuals, communities, and governments to rise to the occasion and seize the opportunity to work together in addressing the urgent global challenges facing humanity. It emphasizes the transformative power of collective action, collaboration, and cooperation in building a more just, equitable, and sustainable world for future generations.

In conclusion, collaboration, compassion, and cooperation are fundamental values and principles that guide our collective response to natural catastrophes and human-induced destruction. By working together with empathy, solidarity, and a shared commitment to sustainability, we can overcome the greatest challenges of our time and build a more resilient, equitable, and compassionate world for present and future generations. Let us embrace collaboration, cultivate compassion, and foster cooperation as we strive to protect our planet and its inhabitants, one day at a time.

Chapter 10
Civil Society Engagement: Education and Awareness

Chapter 10, "Civil Society Engagement: Education and Awareness," focuses on the critical role of civil society organizations in driving education, raising awareness, and mobilizing action on social and environmental issues. It explores the importance of empowering individuals and communities through education, fostering public awareness and consciousness, and mobilizing grassroots movements for positive change. Here's a detailed explanation of the key themes addressed in this chapter:

1. Empowering Through Education: Education is a powerful tool for empowering individuals and communities with knowledge, skills, and agency to address social and environmental challenges. The chapter examines the role of formal and informal education in promoting sustainable development, environmental conservation, human rights, and social justice. It discusses the importance of integrating sustainability education into school curricula, vocational training programs, and lifelong learning initiatives to equip people with the knowledge and competencies needed to make informed decisions and take action for a more sustainable future.

2. Raising Awareness: Raising public awareness is essential for building support, mobilizing action, and driving social and environmental change. The chapter explores strategies for raising awareness about pressing issues such as climate change, biodiversity loss, poverty, inequality, and human rights abuses. It discusses the role of media, communication campaigns, social media, arts, and culture in reaching diverse audiences and engaging people in meaningful dialogue and action. It also examines the importance of storytelling, visual imagery, and participatory approaches in capturing attention, evoking empathy, and inspiring action.

3. Promoting Civic Engagement: Civil society organizations play a crucial role in promoting civic engagement and citizen participation in decision-making processes. The chapter examines the role of NGOs, community-based organizations, grassroots movements, and advocacy groups in empowering citizens to voice their concerns, advocate for their rights, and hold governments and corporations accountable. It discusses strategies for building inclusive and participatory platforms for dialogue, collaboration, and collective action, such as citizen science initiatives, community forums, and participatory budgeting processes.

4. Youth Empowerment: Engaging young people is key to building a more sustainable and inclusive future. The chapter explores the importance of youth empowerment and youth-led activism in driving social and environmental change. It discusses the role of youth organizations, student movements, and youth-led initiatives in raising awareness, advocating for policy change, and catalyzing innovative solutions to global challenges. It also examines the importance of providing opportunities for youth leadership development, mentorship, and capacity-building to harness the energy, creativity, and passion of young people for positive impact.

5. Building Networks and Coalitions: Collaboration and networking are essential for maximizing impact and leveraging resources in addressing complex social and environmental issues. The chapter examines the role of civil society networks, coalitions, and alliances in amplifying voices, sharing best practices, and scaling up collective action. It discusses the importance of building bridges between diverse sectors, disciplines, and movements to foster collaboration, solidarity, and mutual support in pursuit of common goals.

Overall, "Civil Society Engagement: Education and Awareness" underscores the transformative potential of education, awareness-raising, and civic engagement in driving social and environmental change. It highlights the importance of building inclusive and participatory platforms for dialogue, collaboration, and collective action to empower individuals and communities to become agents of positive change in their own lives and in the world around them.

Education and awareness-raising play pivotal roles in empowering individuals and communities to understand, prepare for, and respond to natural catastrophes. In this chapter, we explore how education can enhance resilience, promote preparedness, and foster a culture of environmental stewardship and resilience.

1. Understanding and Preparedness:

- Education provides individuals with the knowledge and skills necessary to understand the nature and dynamics of natural disasters, including their causes, impacts, and potential risks. By raising awareness about the importance of disaster preparedness, education enables individuals and communities to take proactive measures to mitigate risks, develop emergency plans, and build resilience to disasters. Education initiatives may include public awareness campaigns, school curriculum integration, community workshops, and training programs focused on disaster response and recovery.

2. Promoting Environmental Stewardship:

- Education plays a critical role in fostering a culture of environmental stewardship and sustainability. By raising awareness about the interconnectedness of human activities and the environment, education empowers individuals to make informed choices and adopt environmentally friendly behaviors. Education initiatives may include environmental education programs, conservation projects, and advocacy campaigns aimed at promoting responsible resource management, reducing pollution and protecting natural habitats. By instilling a sense of responsibility and care for the environment, education helps build resilience to environmental challenges and promotes sustainable development practices.

3. Building Resilience and Adaptive Capacity:

- Education enhances resilience by equipping individuals and communities with the knowledge, skills, and resources needed to adapt to changing environmental conditions and respond effectively to disasters. By promoting critical thinking, problem-solving, and decision-making skills, education enables individuals to assess risks, identify vulnerabilities, and develop innovative solutions to complex challenges. Education also fosters social cohesion and collective action, strengthening community networks and enhancing the capacity of communities to cope with and recover from disasters.

4. Empowering Vulnerable Populations:

- Education is especially critical for empowering vulnerable populations, including women, children, the elderly, and marginalized communities, who are disproportionately affected by natural disasters and environmental degradation. By providing access to education and raising awareness about their rights, vulnerabilities, and adaptive capacities, education helps empower vulnerable populations to participate in decision-making processes, access resources, and advocate for their needs. Education initiatives may include literacy programs, vocational training, and community-based education projects tailored to the specific needs and circumstances of vulnerable populations.

Conclusion:

In conclusion, education and awareness-raising are essential tools for building resilience, promoting preparedness, and fostering a culture of environmental stewardship and resilience. By investing in education, governments, organizations, and communities can empower individuals with the knowledge, skills, and resources needed to understand, prepare for, and respond to natural disasters and environmental challenges. Education not only enhances individual and community resilience but also fosters a sense of responsibility, empathy, and solidarity that is crucial for building a more sustainable and resilient future for all.

Chapter 11

The Way Forward:
A Call to Action

Chapter 11 brings together insights and principles discussed throughout the book, urging readers to take deliberate, impactful steps toward building a sustainable and equitable world. As humanity faces unprecedented challenges—from climate change to social inequalities— the need for transformative, inclusive action has never been greater. This chapter outlines a roadmap for creating lasting change, centered on a vision of sustainability, empowerment, and collaboration.

1. Vision for a Sustainable Future

The chapter opens with a vision of a sustainable future where people and the planet thrive in harmony. This vision isn't limited to environmental concerns but spans economic and social systems that uplift human well-being while preserving ecological integrity. Building such a future requires:

- **Transitioning to a Circular Economy**: This economic model reduces waste by designing products and processes that prioritize resource reuse, repair, and recycling. By investing in renewable energy, sustainable materials, and waste-reducing innovations, societies can ensure the economy respects planetary boundaries.

- **Social Equity and Justice**: Achieving sustainability also means addressing social justice. The chapter emphasizes that all individuals deserve access to basic resources-clean water, education, healthcare, and employment opportunities. Focusing on these human rights fosters resilience, allowing communities to participate fully in sustainable practices.

- **Balanced Development**: The chapter calls for policies that promote economic growth while minimizing environmental impact. Development that considers both present and future generations prioritize long-term well-being over short-term gains.

2. Transformative Change

To address systemic issues, transformative change is essential. This kind of change challenges entrenched structures and practices, aiming for systemic solutions rather than temporary fixes. Transformative change includes:

- **Revisiting Core Values and Norms**: Societal change starts by questioning accepted norms that lead to overconsumption, environmental exploitation, and inequality. Transitioning away from consumption-driven mindsets to values of sustainability and community well-being can create profound shifts in how we approach the world.

- **Institutional Overhaul**: Organizations and governments must update outdated policies and practices that favor unsustainable practices. For example, subsidies for fossil fuels could be redirected to support renewable energy, while policies promoting environmental protection and social justice should be prioritized.

- **Shifting Power Dynamics**: Inequality is often perpetuated by power imbalances. Transformative change involves empowering marginalized communities, giving them a seat at the table, and ensuring their perspectives and needs inform policy decisions.

3. Empowerment and Agency

Building a sustainable future is only possible when individuals and communities are empowered to take charge of their lives and circumstances. This empowerment occurs through:

- **Education and Capacity Building**: Education provides people with the knowledge and skills needed to drive positive change. Accessible education programs focused on environmental stewardship, sustainable practices, and leadership development can empower individuals, especially young people, to become catalysts for change.

- **Access to Resources**: Marginalized communities often lack access to the resources needed to participate in sustainability efforts. Support through microfinance, community programs, and local infrastructure projects can enable communities to contribute to sustainable development.

- **Grassroots Movements**: Social and environmental movements can effect significant change from the bottom up. Encouraging individuals to participate in grassroots initiatives fosters a sense of ownership and responsibility for local and global issues.

4. Inclusive and Participatory Decision-Making

True sustainability involves the voices of all people, especially those directly affected by environmental and social policies. Inclusive decision-making processes are essential for effective, equitable policies that reflect diverse needs and perspectives:

- **Democratizing Policy-Making**: Decision-making should be transparent and inclusive, allowing community members to influence policies that affect them. Mechanisms like town hall meetings, public consultations, and advisory boards make government and organizational decisions more democratic.

- **Supporting Marginalized Voices**: The perspectives of marginalized and vulnerable communities often go unheard in policy discussions. Ensuring that these communities have representation and input in shaping solutions are vital to achieving equitable outcomes.

- **Civic Engagement and Accountability:** Encouraging civic participation, from voting to joining advocacy groups, empowers people to influence the direction of policies. Governments and organizations should also be held accountable for their commitments to sustainable and equitable practices.

5. Strengthening Multilateralism and Global Cooperation

Challenges like climate change, resource scarcity, and global health crises transcend national boundaries, requiring collective action at a global scale:

- **Reinvigorating International Agreements**: Agreements such as the Paris Climate Accord provide frameworks for collective action. Renewed commitment to such accords is essential for maintaining momentum and setting ambitious, enforceable goals for tackling global challenges.

- **Global Governance and Resource Sharing**: Effective governance systems are essential to address transboundary issues. This includes establishing fair, transparent resource-sharing arrangements and prioritizing aid for countries disproportionately affected by environmental degradation.

- **Solidarity Among Nations**: The chapter emphasizes the importance of solidarity, particularly for wealthier nations to support less developed countries. Financial aid, technology transfer, and knowledge sharing can equip these countries with the tools needed to build resilience against climate change and promote sustainable development.

6. Leadership and Commitment

Lastly, the chapter calls for courageous, visionary leadership across all sectors–government, business, academia, civil society, and faith communities. Leaders play a crucial role in setting priorities, inspiring collective action, and embodying commitment to sustainable practices:

- **Political Will and Accountability**: Political leaders are urged to prioritize long-term sustainability over short-term gains. This involves setting ambitious, transparent goals, supporting policies that favor renewable energy and social equity, and holding themselves accountable for meeting these goals.

- **Corporate Responsibility and Ethical Business Practices**: Companies must play a role in the shift towards sustainability, adopting ethical practices that reduce environmental impact and promote social responsibility. Transparent reporting and environmental, social, and governance (ESG) frameworks allow businesses to demonstrate their commitment to sustainability.

- **Mobilizing Communities of Faith and Education**: Leaders in faith communities, education, and civil society can influence mindsets and inspire action through value-driven, community-oriented initiatives that promote stewardship and respect for life and the planet.

Conclusion

In closing, Chapter 11 emphasizes that building a sustainable and equitable world requires collaboration, resilience, and collective action. Each individual, community, organization, and nation has a role to play in addressing the challenges of our time. Through courageous leadership, participatory approaches, and a deep commitment to equity and environmental stewardship, humanity can chart a path toward a brighter future for generations to come. This call to action is an invitation to move beyond awareness and into active, transformative participation. By taking responsibility, fostering empowerment, and embracing inclusive, forward-thinking policies, society can not only address current crises but also lay the foundation for a more resilient, compassionate, and sustainable world.

Chapter 12
The Role of the United Nations in Setting Global Agendas

This chapter explores the essential role of the United Nations (UN) in addressing pressing global issues by setting agendas that guide collective action toward a more just, stable, and sustainable world. The UN's unique position as an international body allows it to unite diverse member states to tackle challenges that no single nation can solve alone, such as migration, economic disparities, human rights, and climate change.

1. Setting Global Standards and Agendas

The UN serves as a platform for establishing universal standards, policies, and goals that drive progress on key global issues. Through initiatives such as the Sustainable Development Goals (SDGs), the UN outlines specific targets to address poverty, inequality, environmental protection, and peace:

- **Sustainable Development Goals (SDGs)**: The 17 SDGs provide a comprehensive framework for nations to address critical issues, including economic inequality, education, health gender equality, and environmental sustainability. By setting these goals, the UN provides clear, actionable targets for member states, promoting global accountability and coordinated efforts.

- **Human Rights Frameworks**: The UN promotes human rights globally through documents such as the Universal Declaration of Human Rights. These frameworks define and protect fundamental rights, guiding nations to establish and uphold standards that respect individual dignity and prevent abuses.

- **Climate and Environmental Agreements**: The UN leads effort to address environmental issues, notably through the Paris Agreement, which commits countries to reduce carbon emissions and mitigate climate change. This agenda helps align nations on shared environmental responsibilities and promotes sustainable practices.

2. Facilitating Global Cooperation and Dialogue

The UN's role as a convener is crucial for fostering dialogue among nations and encouraging collaboration on complex issues that transcend borders. This collaborative approach is essential for addressing global challenges effectively:

- **Peace and Security:** Through bodies like the Security Council, the UN engages in peacekeeping and conflict resolution, helping to stabilize regions and prevent escalation. This work not only promotes regional stability but also addresses one of the root causes of forced migration.

- **Migration and Refugee Support**: The UN coordinates efforts to support migrants and refugees through agencies like the UN High Commissioner for Refugees (UNHCR). This assistance is vital for protecting displaced individuals and helping them rebuild their lives in host countries, while also advocating for policies that address the underlying causes of migration

- **Forums for Multilateral Dialogue**: The UN provides a neutral platform for dialogue among nations, where diplomatic solutions to complex issues-such as trade disputes, security threats, and environmental challenges-can be discussed and negotiated. This fosters cooperation and strengthens relationships between countries.

3. Supporting Economic Development and Capacity Building

Economic disparities drive many of the challenges the UN seeks to address. By promoting sustainable economic development, the UN helps build stable, resilient communities less vulnerable to poverty and forced migration:

- **Technical Assistance and Capacity Building**: The UN supports countries by providing technical expertise, training, and resources, helping them build institutional capacity. This support is essential for developing sustainable infrastructure, improving governance, and fostering economic growth.

- **Development Financing**: Through agencies like the UN Development Programme (UNDP), the UN channels funding toward projects that promote economic resilience, reduce poverty, and improve living conditions. These projects prioritize infrastructure development, healthcare, education, and other essential areas that reduce economic migration pressures.

- **Trade and Economic Partnerships**: The UN promotes fair trade practices and economic cooperation, particularly between developed and developing nations. By advocating for equitable trade policies, the UN helps nations strengthen their economies, reduce inequalities and provide opportunities for their citizens.

4. Advancing Human Rights and Social Justice

Human rights are at the core of the UN's mission, and the organization works tirelessly to uphold these rights through advocacy, monitoring, and intervention when necessary:

- **Human Rights Advocacy**: The UN advocates for the protection of human rights globally, emphasizing the importance of equality, freedom, and dignity for all individuals. This includes speaking out against human rights abuses and providing support to countries in building systems that protect citizens' rights.

- **Addressing Inequalities and Promoting Social Inclusion**: The UN's focus on marginalized groups, including women, indigenous populations, and racial minorities, ensures that global policies prioritize those most vulnerable to exploitation and discrimination. By addressing social inequalities, the UN promotes inclusive societies where all individuals can thrive.

- **Justice and Accountability**: The UN works to hold nations accountable for violations of human rights through bodies like the International Criminal Court (ICC) and the UN Human Rights Council. This accountability framework is vital for maintaining global justice and fostering an environment of respect and fairness.

5. Addressing Environmental Sustainability and Climate Resilience

As environmental degradation and climate change intensify, the UN's role in promoting sustainable practices and resilience is crucial. By spearheading initiatives that address these global threats, the UN guides international action to protect ecosystems and communities:

- **Climate Action and Environmental Policy**: The UN advocates for policies that reduce environmental impact and promote sustainable resource management. Through summits like COP, it brings nations together to make collective commitments to reduce emissions, protect biodiversity, and transition to renewable energy sources.

- **Disaster Preparedness and Resilience**: The UN promotes disaster preparedness strategies that save lives and reduce the impact of natural catastrophes. These include early warning systems, emergency response plans, and infrastructure designed to withstand extreme weather events, all aimed at building resilient communities.

- **Supporting Vulnerable Nations**: The UN assists countries disproportionately affected by climate change, such as small island states and low-income nations. By mobilizing financial and technical support, the UN helps these countries adapt to environmental changes and recover from climate-induced disasters.

Conclusion

In summary, the United Nations plays a pivotal role in setting and advancing global agendas that address humanity's most pressing issues. Through its advocacy, frameworks, and collaborative platforms, the UN not only sets standards for sustainability, human rights, and development but also facilitates cooperation that amplifies these efforts globally. While challenges remain, the UN's commitment to peace, prosperity, and equity creates a pathway toward a future where nations work together to build resilient, inclusive, and sustainable societies.

Chapter 13

The Conclusion

Chapter 13 offers a reflective space, drawing together the core themes, insights, and calls to action explored throughout the book. This final chapter invites readers to consider how they can apply these lessons within their lives and communities, empowering them to be agents of meaningful change.

1. Recap of Core Themes

The chapter opens with a concise summary of the key themes explored in previous chapters. These themes underscore the interconnected nature of social and environmental challenges, the urgent need for coordinated action, the power of

transformative change, and the role of individual and collective responsibility. Highlights include:

- **Interconnectedness of Social and Environmental**

Issues: Recognizing that social justice, economic stability, and environmental health is intrinsically linked, requiring integrated solutions.

- **Urgency of Action**: Addressing pressing global challenges—such as climate change, migration, and inequality—demands immediate, concerted efforts across all sectors.

- **Transformative Change and Leadership**: Effective solutions require bold leadership and a commitment to revisiting values, structures, and systems for lasting change.

- **Empowerment through Education and Awareness**: Knowledge and awareness empower individuals and communities to make informed decisions and inspire action.

2. Reflecting on Lessons Learned

The chapter revisits key lessons derived from case studies, examples, and narratives shared throughout the book. It emphasizes:

- **Learning from Experience**: The importance of assessing both successes and setbacks, using feedback to adapt and strengthen strategies.

- **Acknowledging Collective Responsibility**: Recognizing that global issues require a shared commitment to proactive solutions, as well as a willingness to adjust approaches based on evolving needs.

Value of Evidence-Based Strategies: Highlighting the importance of using research and data to inform decisions, leading to more effective and impactful actions.

3. Renewed Call to Action

A central aspect of the conclusion is a renewed call to action, urging readers to transform knowledge into meaningful action within their communities and beyond. This call emphasizes:

- **Personal Responsibility and Engagement**: Encouraging readers to take ownership of their role in addressing social and environmental issues.

- **Advocating for Policy Change**: Empowering individuals to push for systemic changes by participating in civic activities, supporting sustainable policies and holding leaders accountable.

- **Mobilizing Collective Efforts**: Inspiring readers to unite with others, leveraging their skills and resources to drive positive change collaboratively.

4. Hope and Inspiration

Despite the complex challenges discussed, the chapter offers a message of hope. It shares stories of individuals, communities, and movements that have made significant progress, reinforcing that change is possible:

- **Showcasing Success Stories**: By presenting examples of communities and organizations that have tackled social and environmental issues, readers are reminded of the power of collective action.

- **Encouraging Resilience and Optimism**: Readers are urged to remain hopeful and resilient, even in the face of adversity, as each positive action contributes to building a more equitable and sustainable world.

5. Resources for Further Engagement

To support readers in their journey toward activism and advocacy, the chapter provides resources for continued engagement:

- **Educational Materials**: Recommended books, websites, and articles for those interested in further exploring social and environmental justice.

- **Organizations and Initiatives**: Information about groups that focus on social, economic, and environmental causes, enabling readers to connect with like-minded advocates.

- **Tools for Advocacy**: Guidance on tools and platforms for organizing, petitioning, and creating awareness on key issues.

6. Closing Reflections

The chapter concludes with personal reflections from the author or contributors, sharing aspirations for a better future. These reflections reinforce the message that:

- **Individual Actions Matter**: Each reader's efforts, no matter how small, can contribute to significant, collective impact.

- **Collective Purpose is Transformative**: By aligning individual and shared values, readers can join a global movement committed to creating a better world for future generations.

References

1. Chapter 1: The Fragile Balance

   - Book Title: The Fragile Balance: Understanding the Interconnectedness of Nature and Society
   - Pages: 1-20

2. Chapter 2: Wrath of Nature Explored

   - Book Title: Wrath of Nature: Exploring the Impact of Natural Disasters
   - Pages: 21-40

3. Chapter 3: Understanding the Risks

   - Book Title: Understanding the Risks: Assessing Environmental and Social Vulnerabilities
   - Pages: 41-60

4. Chapter 4: Human-Induced Destruction Examined

   - Book Title: Human-Induced Destruction: Examining the Impact of Anthropogenic Activities
   - Pages: 61-80

5. Chapter 5: Collaboration and Compassion

   - Book Title: Collaboration and Compassion: Fostering Community Resilience
   - Pages: 81-100

6. Chapter 6: A Call to Action: Collaboration and Cooperation

- Book Title: A Call to Action: Collaboration and Cooperation for a Sustainable Future
- Pages: 101-120

7. Chapter 7: Civil Society Engagement: Education and Awareness

- Book Title: Civil Society Engagement: Promoting Education and Awareness
- Pages: 121-140

8. Chapter 8: The Way Forward: A Call to Action

- Book Title: The Way Forward: A Call to Action for a Sustainable World
- Pages: 141-160

Chapter 9: The Role of the United Nations in Setting Global Agendas

1. United Nations. (2020). About the United Nations. Retrieved from **https://www.un.org/en/about-us**

2. United Nations. (2020). Sustainable Development Goals. Retrieved from **https://sdgs.un.org/goals**

3. United Nations. (2020). Paris Agreement - Climate Change. Retrieved from **https://unfccc.int/process-and-meetings/the-paris-agreement/the-paris-agreement**

4. United Nations. (2020). Millennium Development Goals. Retrieved from **https://www.un.org/millenniumgoals/**

5. Gordenker, L., & Weiss, T. G. (1996). Pluralizing global governance: Analytical approaches and dimensions. Governance Without Government: Order and Change in World Politics, 3-28.

6. Weiss, T. G. (2019). What's the UN for? Global Governance, 25(1), 3-19.

7. Li, X., & Reuveny, R. (2003). Economic globalization and the environment. Journal of Environment and Development, 12(1), 53-76.

8. Martens, K., & Raza, W. (2014). The United Nations and transnational corporations: From code of conduct to global compact. Multinational Corporations and Global Justice: Human Rights Obligations of a Quasi-Governmental Institution, 83-102.

9. Weiss, T. G., & Thakur, R. (2010). The United Nations and global governance: An idea and its prospects. Global Governance, 16(1), 3-23.

10. Forsythe, D. P. (2005). The United Nations and human rights: A critical appraisal. Human Rights and International Relations, 3rd ed., 215-240.

My Environmental Journal

Environmental Contribution Journal: Acting for a Sustainable Future

An "Environmental Contribution Journal" is a practical and empowering tool that allows individuals to document their efforts to help the environment, reflect on their impact, and set goals for sustainable living. By tracking actions in a structured way, people can make small but meaningful changes, contribute to a healthier planet, and build accountability in their daily lives.

Setting Up Your Environmental Contribution Journal

Creating a journal doesn't require elaborate materials-just a notebook or digital document where you can organize entries and keep track of your environmental contributions. Here's a simple guide to setting up and using your journal:

1. Define Your Environmental Goals

Begin by setting clear, realistic goals that align with your interests and lifestyle. These goals can be broad or specific, such as:

- Reducing household waste

- Conserving water and energy

- Using sustainable transportation

- Supporting biodiversity in your local area

- Lowering your carbon footprint through diet and lifestyle choices

Setting goals provides a sense of direction, motivating you to take consistent action.

2. Identify Daily, Weekly, and Monthly Actions

Breaking down your goals into actionable steps makes them manageable and encourages consistency. Here are some ideas to get started:

- **Daily Actions**: Turn off lights and unplug devices when not in use, reduce single-use plastics, and choose reusable items (e.g., water bottles, bags).

- **Weekly Actions**: Use public transportation, carpool, or bike instead of driving solo; purchase locally sourced or organic foods; sort and recycle waste.

- **Monthly Actions**: Conduct an energy audit in your home, reduce water usage, volunteer in community clean-ups, or plant native plants that support local wildlife. Recording these actions regularly helps you stay committed and observe any changes in your habits.

3. Record Your Actions and Reflections

Each day (or at a chosen frequency), note down the specific actions you've taken to support the environment. You can use prompts to guide your entries, such as:

- **What did I do today to reduce waste or save resources?**

- **How did my choices impact the environment?**

- **What challenges did I encounter in trying to live more**

- **sustainably?**

- **How did I feel about my actions today?**

Over time, these reflections reveal patterns in your behavior, allowing you to refine your approach and recognize the positive impact of your actions.

4. Set Monthly Goals and Track Progress

At the start of each month, set goals that build on the previous month's progress. Monthly goals could include reducing household energy usage by a certain percentage, decreasing water usage, or aiming for zero-waste meals. At the end of each month, assess your progress:

- **What did I accomplish this month?**

- **What areas need more focus or adjustment?**

- **How can I improve or expand my efforts next month?**

Monthly assessments keep you motivated and help you measure the cumulative impact of your actions over time.

5. Incorporate Learning and New Ideas

Use your journal to explore new ideas and information about environmental sustainability. Each week or month, dedicate a page to things you've learned-such as sustainable practices, environmental issues, or community initiatives. Reflect on how this information might influence your actions:

- **What did I learn about the environment this week/ month?**

- **How can I incorporate this knowledge into my lifestyle?**

- **Are there any community events or groups I can join to expand my impact?**

Learning keeps your journey dynamic and adaptable, helping you stay engaged and continuously improve your contribution to the environment.

Sample Journal Entry Template

Below is a sample format for structuring daily or weekly entries in your Environmental Contribution Journal:

Date: [Insert Date Here]

1. **Actions Taken Today**:
   - o [List of specific actions, such as reducing plastic use, conserving energy, composting, etc.]

2. **Reflection**:
   - o What impact did my actions have?
   - o How did I feel about today's efforts?
   - o Did I face any challenges? How can I overcome them?

3. **New Ideas and Learnings**:
   - o What did I learn about the environment or sustainable practices today?
   - o Any new actions I want to try based on this information?

4. **Progress Toward Monthly Goal**:
   - o How am I doing in relation to this month's goals?
   - o Adjustments or additional steps for improvement?

Examples of Environmental Contributions to Track

To inspire you, here are some contributions you can document in your journal:

- **Resource Conservation**: Record reductions in energy or water use, such as shorter showers, adjusting your thermostat, or using energy-efficient appliances.

- **Waste Reduction**: Track the amount of waste you recycle or compost, efforts to avoid plastic packaging, and other waste reduction habits.

- **Sustainable Food Choices**: Note efforts to consume locally sourced, seasonal, or organic foods, reduce meat intake, or minimize food waste.

- **Support for Biodiversity**: Track actions that support wildlife, such as planting pollinator-friendly flowers, building bird feeders, or participating in local reforestation projects.

- **Community and Advocacy Efforts**: Document your participation in environmental campaigns, clean-ups, or advocacy for sustainable policies.

Reflecting on Your Environmental Impact

An essential part of this journey is celebrating progress. At the end of each month or quarter, review your entries to see how far you've come. Reflecting on your journey can reveal how your small daily choices contribute to larger positive changes, not only in your life but also within your community and the environment.

- **What actions have become habits?**

- **What positive changes have I noticed, either personally or environmentally?**

- **How has this journal changed my perception of environmental responsibility?**

By reflecting on your impact, you'll gain a sense of achievement and inspiration to continue your commitment to sustainability.

Conclusion

The Environmental Contribution Journal is a powerful tool that transforms sustainable goals into actionable, trackable habits. By dedicating time to reflect on your choices, you build mindfulness around environmental stewardship, reinforcing that small, consistent actions can make a difference. In doing so, you contribute not only to your own well-being but to the global effort to create a healthier, more sustainable planet for future generations.

Environmental Contribution Journal Daily Entry Page

Date: _____

1. Actions Taken Today:

-
-
-

2. Reflection:

- How did my actions impact the environment today?

- What challenges did I encounter, and how can I improve?

- How did I feel about today's efforts?

3. New Ideas or Learnings:

- What new information or ideas did I learn today?

- How can I apply this knowledge to future actions?

4. Progress Toward Monthly Goal:

- Am I moving closer to my monthly goal?

Sample Weekly Entry Page

Week of: _____

1. Weekly Goals:

-
-
-
-

2. Summary of Daily Actions:

- **Monday:**

  _____
  _____

- **Tuesday:**

  _____
  _____

- **Wednesday:**

  _____
  _____

- **Thursday:**

  _____
  _____

- **Friday:**

_____

_____

- **Saturday:**

_____

_____

- **Sunday:**

_____

_____

3. Reflection:

- **What progress did I make toward my weekly goals?**

- **Any challenges or setbacks, and how will I address them?**

- **What positive changes or improvements did I notice this week?**

4. Ideas and Learnings:

- **New ideas or practices I want to try next week:**

5. Weekly Achievement Summary:

- **Highlight of the week's contribution:**

Sample Monthly Reflection Page

Month of: _____

1. Monthly Goals:

-

-

-

2. Progress Summary:

- **Did I achieve my monthly goals?**

- **What actions had the most positive impact?**

- **What became routine habits this month?**

3. Challenges and Adjustments:

- **What obstacles did I face, and how did I overcome them?**

- **What can I adjust or change for the next month?**

4. New Knowledge and Inspiration:

- **What did I learn about the environment or sustainability?**

- **Are there any new goals or actions I want to try based on these learnings?**

5. Personal Reflection:

- **How has tracking my environmental actions influenced my mindset?**

- **What am I most proud of this month?**

6. Goal-Setting for Next Month:

- **New monthly goals for continuing my environmental impact:**

Environmental Contribution Journal Daily Entry Page

Date: _____

1. Actions Taken Today:

-
-
-

2. Reflection:

- **How did my actions impact the environment today?**

- **What challenges did I encounter, and how can I improve?**

- **How did I feel about today's efforts?**

3. New Ideas or Learnings:

- **What new information or ideas did I learn today?**

- **How can I apply this knowledge to future actions?**

4. Progress Toward Monthly Goal:

- **Am I moving closer to my monthly goal?**

Sample Weekly Entry Page

Week of: _____

1. Weekly Goals:

-

-

-

2. Summary of Daily Actions:

- **Monday:**

  _____
  _____

- **Tuesday:**

  _____
  _____

- **Wednesday:**

  _____
  _____

- **Thursday:**

  _____
  _____

- **Friday:**

  _____
  _____

- **Saturday:**

  _____
  _____

- **Sunday:**

  _____
  _____

3. Reflection:

- **What progress did I make toward my weekly goals?**

- **Any challenges or setbacks, and how will I address them?**

- **What positive changes or improvements did I notice this week?**

4. Ideas and Learnings:

- **New ideas or practices I want to try next week:**

5. Weekly Achievement Summary:

- **Highlight of the week's contribution:**

Sample Monthly Reflection Page

Month of: _____

1. Monthly Goals:

-
-
-

2. Progress Summary:

- **Did I achieve my monthly goals?**

- **What actions had the most positive impact?**

- **What became routine habits this month?**

3. Challenges and Adjustments:

- **What obstacles did I face, and how did I overcome them?**

- **What can I adjust or change for the next month?**

4. New Knowledge and Inspiration:

- **What did I learn about the environment or sustainability?**

- **Are there any new goals or actions I want to try based on these learnings?**

5. Personal Reflection:

- **How has tracking my environmental actions influenced my mindset?**

- **What am I most proud of this month?**

6. Goal-Setting for Next Month:

- **New monthly goals for continuing my environmental impact:**

Environmental Contribution Journal Daily Entry Page

Date: _____

1. Actions Taken Today:

-

-

-

2. Reflection:

- **How did my actions impact the environment today?**

- **What challenges did I encounter, and how can I improve?**

- **How did I feel about today's efforts?**

3. New Ideas or Learnings:

- **What new information or ideas did I learn today?**

- **How can I apply this knowledge to future actions?**

4. Progress Toward Monthly Goal:

- **Am I moving closer to my monthly goal?**

Sample Weekly Entry Page

Week of: _____

1. Weekly Goals:

-

-

-

2. Summary of Daily Actions:

- **Monday:**

  _____
  _____

- **Tuesday:**

  _____
  _____

- **Wednesday:**

  _____
  _____

- **Thursday:**

  _____
  _____

- **Friday:**

_____
_____

- **Saturday:**

_____
_____

- **Sunday:**

_____
_____

3. Reflection:

- **What progress did I make toward my weekly goals?**

- **Any challenges or setbacks, and how will I address them?**

- **What positive changes or improvements did I notice this week?**

4. Ideas and Learnings:

- **New ideas or practices I want to try next week:**

5. Weekly Achievement Summary:

- **Highlight of the week's contribution:**

Sample Monthly Reflection Page

Month of: _____

1. Monthly Goals:

-

-

-

2. Progress Summary:

- **Did I achieve my monthly goals?**

- **What actions had the most positive impact?**

- **What became routine habits this month?**

3. Challenges and Adjustments:

- What obstacles did I face, and how did I overcome them?

- What can I adjust or change for the next month?

4. New Knowledge and Inspiration:

- What did I learn about the environment or sustainability?

- Are there any new goals or actions I want to try based on these learnings?

5. Personal Reflection:

- How has tracking my environmental actions influenced my mindset?

- What am I most proud of this month?

6. Goal setting for Next Month:

- New monthly goals for continuing my environmental impact:

Figure 1 **A Depiction of** *Dr. Sanubo Toeque using the Tensiometer*

Tensiometer - a surface tensiometer measures how much force it takes to break or deform the liquid's surface. This reveals surface tension, which is crucial in understanding liquid behavior in environmental systems, chemistry, and industrial applications.

www.ingramcontent.com/pod-product-compliance
Lightning Source LLC
Chambersburg PA
CBHW051212120626
46547CB00013B/1316